THIS JOURNAL BELONGS TO:

____

____

YOU MUST GAIN CONTROL OVER YOUR MONEY, OR THE LACK OF IT WILL FOREVER CONTROL YOU.

DAVE RAMSEY

Thank You
FOR SUPPORTING MY SMALL BUSINESS!
WE HOPE OUR PRODUCT
BRIGHTENED YOUR DAY.
YOUR SUPPORT MADE OURS!
FOR FUTURE PRODUCT ANNOUNCEMENTS AND DISCOUNTS FOLLOW US ON SOCIAL MEDIA
www.gracefulbydesign.com
@gracefulbydesignllc
Graceful BY DESIGN
ELEGANT ORGANIZATION FOR EVERYDAY LIFE
Jenna

TABLE OF CONTENTS

5 FINANCIALS GOALS FOR THIS YEAR

GOAL #1

SUPPORTING GOAL:

GOAL #2

SUPPORTING GOAL:

GOAL #3

SUPPORTING GOAL:

GOAL #4

SUPPORTING GOAL:

GOAL #5

SUPPORTING GOAL:

VISION BOARD FOR THE YEAR

GOAL EXAMPLE *Reduce monthly spending by $800*

NEW SKILLS NEEDED TO ACHIEVE THIS GOAL	
make coffee at home	coupon and check sales
plan and meal prep ahead	Trade in car for lower car payment option
track spending habits daily	reduce utilities
revaluate ALL subscription costs	

ACTIONS TO ACHIEVE THIS GOAL

- Limit getting coffee out to once per month.
- Pack lunches for work
- Order take-out once per week
- Set a time each day to fill in my budget journal.
- Check all subscription & regular bills on credit cards
- Check thermostat often & hang dry cloths

TARGET DATE TO REACH THIS GOAL:

MY REWARD FOR REACHING THIS GOAL:

GOAL #1

NEW SKILLS NEEDED TO ACHIEVE THIS GOAL

ACTIONS TO ACHIEVE THIS GOAL

TARGET DATE TO REACH THIS GOAL:

MY REWARD FOR REACHING THIS GOAL:

GOAL #2

NEW SKILLS NEEDED TO ACHIEVE THIS GOAL

ACTIONS TO ACHIEVE THIS GOAL

TARGET DATE TO REACH THIS GOAL:

MY REWARD FOR REACHING THIS GOAL:

GOAL #3

NEW SKILLS NEEDED TO ACHIEVE THIS GOAL

ACTIONS TO ACHIEVE THIS GOAL

TARGET DATE TO REACH THIS GOAL:

MY REWARD FOR REACHING THIS GOAL:

GOAL #4

NEW SKILLS NEEDED TO ACHIEVE THIS GOAL

ACTIONS TO ACHIEVE THIS GOAL

TARGET DATE TO REACH THIS GOAL:

MY REWARD FOR REACHING THIS GOAL:

GOAL #5

NEW SKILLS NEEDED TO ACHIEVE THIS GOAL

ACTIONS TO ACHIEVE THIS GOAL

TARGET DATE TO REACH THIS GOAL:

MY REWARD FOR REACHING THIS GOAL:

IMPORTANT DATES

JANUARY

FEBRUARY

MARCH

APRIL

MAY

JUNE

IMPORTANT DATES

JULY

AUGUST

SEPTEMBER

OCTOBER

NOVEMBER

DECEMBER

VACATION BUDGET

CATEGORY	BUDGETED	ACTUAL
SUBTOTAL		

TOTAL BUDGETED	TOTAL ACTUAL	DIFFERENCE

HOLIDAY GIFTS & SPENDING

CATEGORY	BUDGETED	ACTUAL
SUBTOTAL		

TOTAL BUDGETED	TOTAL ACTUAL	DIFFERENCE

BIRTHDAYS

RECIPIENT	CATEGORY	BUDGETED	ACTUAL
	SUBTOTAL		

TOTAL BUDGETED	TOTAL ACTUAL	DIFFERENCE

"A BUDGET IS TELLING YOUR MONEY WHERE TO GO INSTEAD OF WONDERING WHERE IT WENT."

DAVE RAMSEY

MONTH 1

MONTH & YEAR:

MAIN GOALS THIS MONTH *in order of priority*

FINANCIAL TO-DO LIST

INCOME	AMOUNT	DATE

SAVINGS	AMOUNT	DATE

SUN	MON	TUE	WED	THU	FRI	SAT

MONTH 1

MONTHLY BUDGET

	EXPENSE	BUDGETED	ACTUAL
HOUSING	MORTAGE/RENT		
	INSURANCE		
	MAINTENANCE		
	ELECTRICITY		
	WATER/SEWER		
	GAS/HEATING		
	TRASH		
	PHONE		
	TV/INTERNET		
	SUBTOTAL		
FOOD	GROCERIES		
	DINING OUT		
	SUBTOTAL		
HEALTH CARE	INSURANCE		
	MEDICAL		
	SUBTOTAL		
TRANSPORTATION	CAR PAYMENT		
	INSURANCE		
	FUEL		
	MAINTENANCE		
	PUBLIC TRANS		
	SUBTOTAL		

	EXPENSE	BUDGETED	ACTUAL
PERSONAL	CLOTHING		
	PERSONAL CARE		
	SUBTOTAL		
LOANS	CREDIT CARDS		
	SUBTOTAL		
ENTERTAINMENT	EVENTS/GAMES		
	HOBBIES		
	SUBTOTAL		
OTHER			
	SUBTOTAL		

TOTAL BUDGETED	TOTAL ACTUAL	DIFFERENCE

MONTH 1
EXPENSE TRACKER

DATE	DESCRIPTION	CATEGORY	AMOUNT

MONTH 1

EXPENSE TRACKER

DATE	DESCRIPTION	CATEGORY	AMOUNT

MONTH 1

EXPENSE TRACKER

DATE	DESCRIPTION	CATEGORY	AMOUNT

MONTH 1

EXPENSE TRACKER

DATE	DESCRIPTION	CATEGORY	AMOUNT

MONTH 1

BUDGET REVIEW

OPENING BALANCE	
TOTAL INCOME	
TOTAL EXPENSES	
DIFFERENCE	
TOTAL SAVINGS	
BALANCE FORWARD	

SPENDING ANALYSIS

CATEGORY	AMOUNT	%

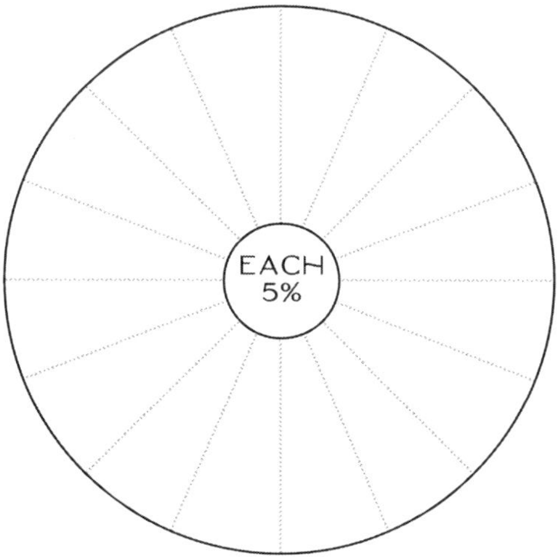

MY BIGGEST WINS THIS MONTH...

DID I MEET MY BUDGET? IF NOT, WHY NOT?

DID I ACHIEVE THIS MONTH'S GOALS? IF NOT, WHY NOT?

WHAT DID I LEARN THIS MONTH FROM TRACKING MY EXPENSES?

MONTH 1

THOUGHTS, NOTES & IDEAS

MONTH 2

MONTH & YEAR:

MAIN GOALS THIS MONTH *in order of priority*

FINANCIAL TO-DO LIST

INCOME	AMOUNT	DATE

SAVINGS	AMOUNT	DATE

SUN	MON	TUE	WED	THU	FRI	SAT

MONTH 2

MONTHLY BUDGET

	EXPENSE	BUDGETED	ACTUAL
HOUSING	MORTAGE/RENT		
	INSURANCE		
	MAINTENANCE		
	ELECTRICITY		
	WATER/SEWER		
	GAS/HEATING		
	TRASH		
	PHONE		
	TV/INTERNET		
	SUBTOTAL		
FOOD	GROCERIES		
	DINING OUT		
	SUBTOTAL		
HEALTH CARE	INSURANCE		
	MEDICAL		
	SUBTOTAL		
TRANSPORTATION	CAR PAYMENT		
	INSURANCE		
	FUEL		
	MAINTENANCE		
	PUBLIC TRANS		
	SUBTOTAL		

	EXPENSE	BUDGETED	ACTUAL
PERSONAL	CLOTHING		
	PERSONAL CARE		
	SUBTOTAL		
LOANS	CREDIT CARDS		
	SUBTOTAL		
ENTERTAINMENT	EVENTS/GAMES		
	HOBBIES		
	SUBTOTAL		
OTHER			
	SUBTOTAL		

TOTAL BUDGETED	TOTAL ACTUAL	DIFFERENCE

MONTH 2

EXPENSE TRACKER

DATE	DESCRIPTION	CATEGORY	AMOUNT

MONTH 2

EXPENSE TRACKER

DATE	DESCRIPTION	CATEGORY	AMOUNT

MONTH 2

EXPENSE TRACKER

DATE	DESCRIPTION	CATEGORY	AMOUNT

MONTH 2

EXPENSE TRACKER

DATE	DESCRIPTION	CATEGORY	AMOUNT

MONTH 2

BUDGET REVIEW

OPENING BALANCE	
TOTAL INCOME	
TOTAL EXPENSES	
DIFFERENCE	
TOTAL SAVINGS	
BALANCE FORWARD	

SPENDING ANALYSIS

CATEGORY	AMOUNT	%

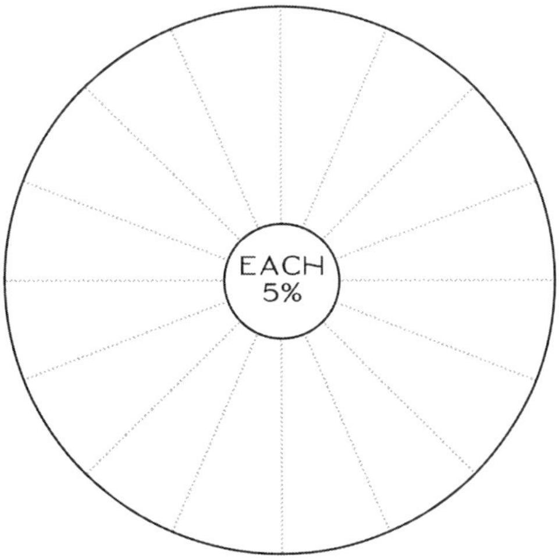

MY BIGGEST WINS THIS MONTH...

DID I MEET MY BUDGET? IF NOT, WHY NOT?

DID I ACHIEVE THIS MONTH'S GOALS? IF NOT, WHY NOT?

WHAT DID I LEARN THIS MONTH FROM TRACKING MY EXPENSES?

MONTH 2

THOUGHTS, NOTES & IDEAS

MONTH 3

MONTH & YEAR:

MAIN GOALS THIS MONTH *in order of priority*

FINANCIAL TO-DO LIST

INCOME	AMOUNT	DATE

SAVINGS	AMOUNT	DATE

SUN	MON	TUE	WED	THU	FRI	SAT

MONTH 3

MONTHLY BUDGET

	EXPENSE	BUDGETED	ACTUAL
HOUSING	MORTAGE/RENT		
	INSURANCE		
	MAINTENANCE		
	ELECTRICITY		
	WATER/SEWER		
	GAS/HEATING		
	TRASH		
	PHONE		
	TV/INTERNET		
	SUBTOTAL		
FOOD	GROCERIES		
	DINING OUT		
	SUBTOTAL		
HEALTH CARE	INSURANCE		
	MEDICAL		
	SUBTOTAL		
TRANSPORTATION	CAR PAYMENT		
	INSURANCE		
	FUEL		
	MAINTENANCE		
	PUBLIC TRANS		
	SUBTOTAL		

	EXPENSE	BUDGETED	ACTUAL
PERSONAL	CLOTHING		
	PERSONAL CARE		
	SUBTOTAL		
LOANS	CREDIT CARDS		
	SUBTOTAL		
ENTERTAINMENT	EVENTS/GAMES		
	HOBBIES		
	SUBTOTAL		
OTHER			
	SUBTOTAL		

TOTAL BUDGETED	TOTAL ACTUAL	DIFFERENCE

MONTH 3

EXPENSE TRACKER

DATE	DESCRIPTION	CATEGORY	AMOUNT

MONTH 3

EXPENSE TRACKER

DATE	DESCRIPTION	CATEGORY	AMOUNT

MONTH 3

EXPENSE TRACKER

DATE	DESCRIPTION	CATEGORY	AMOUNT

MONTH 3
EXPENSE TRACKER

DATE	DESCRIPTION	CATEGORY	AMOUNT

MONTH 3

BUDGET REVIEW

OPENING BALANCE	
TOTAL INCOME	
TOTAL EXPENSES	
DIFFERENCE	
TOTAL SAVINGS	
BALANCE FORWARD	

SPENDING ANALYSIS

CATEGORY	AMOUNT	%

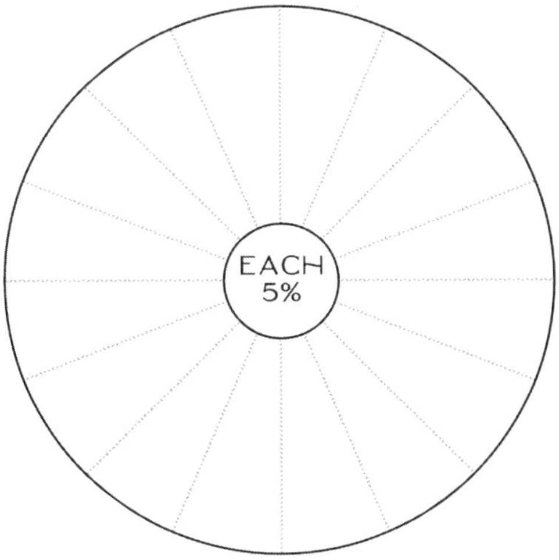

MY BIGGEST WINS THIS MONTH...

DID I MEET MY BUDGET? IF NOT, WHY NOT?

DID I ACHIEVE THIS MONTH'S GOALS? IF NOT, WHY NOT?

WHAT DID I LEARN THIS MONTH FROM TRACKING MY EXPENSES?

THOUGHTS, NOTES & IDEAS

MONTH 4

MONTH & YEAR:

MAIN GOALS THIS MONTH *in order of priority*

FINANCIAL TO-DO LIST

INCOME	AMOUNT	DATE

SAVINGS	AMOUNT	DATE

SUN	MON	TUE	WED	THU	FRI	SAT

MONTH 4

MONTHLY BUDGET

	EXPENSE	BUDGETED	ACTUAL
HOUSING	MORTAGE/RENT		
	INSURANCE		
	MAINTENANCE		
	ELECTRICITY		
	WATER/SEWER		
	GAS/HEATING		
	TRASH		
	PHONE		
	TV/INTERNET		
	SUBTOTAL		
FOOD	GROCERIES		
	DINING OUT		
	SUBTOTAL		
HEALTH CARE	INSURANCE		
	MEDICAL		
	SUBTOTAL		
TRANSPORTATION	CAR PAYMENT		
	INSURANCE		
	FUEL		
	MAINTENANCE		
	PUBLIC TRANS		
	SUBTOTAL		

	EXPENSE	BUDGETED	ACTUAL
PERSONAL	CLOTHING		
	PERSONAL CARE		
	SUBTOTAL		
LOANS	CREDIT CARDS		
	SUBTOTAL		
ENTERTAINMENT	EVENTS/GAMES		
	HOBBIES		
	SUBTOTAL		
OTHER			
	SUBTOTAL		

TOTAL BUDGETED	TOTAL ACTUAL	DIFFERENCE

MONTH 4

EXPENSE TRACKER

DATE	DESCRIPTION	CATEGORY	AMOUNT

MONTH 4

EXPENSE TRACKER

DATE	DESCRIPTION	CATEGORY	AMOUNT

MONTH 4

EXPENSE TRACKER

DATE	DESCRIPTION	CATEGORY	AMOUNT

MONTH 4

EXPENSE TRACKER

DATE	DESCRIPTION	CATEGORY	AMOUNT

MONTH 4

BUDGET REVIEW

OPENING BALANCE	
TOTAL INCOME	
TOTAL EXPENSES	
DIFFERENCE	
TOTAL SAVINGS	
BALANCE FORWARD	

SPENDING ANALYSIS

CATEGORY	AMOUNT	%

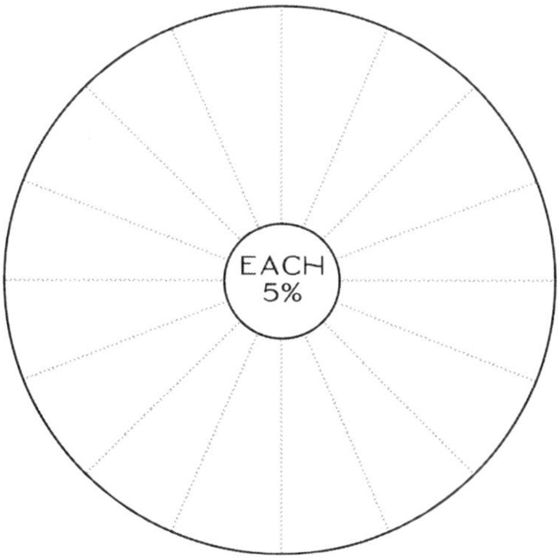

MY BIGGEST WINS THIS MONTH...

DID I MEET MY BUDGET? IF NOT, WHY NOT?

DID I ACHIEVE THIS MONTH'S GOALS? IF NOT, WHY NOT?

WHAT DID I LEARN THIS MONTH FROM TRACKING MY EXPENSES?

MONTH 4

THOUGHTS, NOTES & IDEAS

MONTH 5

MONTH & YEAR:

MAIN GOALS THIS MONTH *in order of priority*

FINANCIAL TO-DO LIST

INCOME	AMOUNT	DATE

SAVINGS	AMOUNT	DATE

SUN	MON	TUE	WED	THU	FRI	SAT

MONTH 5

MONTHLY BUDGET

	EXPENSE	BUDGETED	ACTUAL
HOUSING	MORTAGE/RENT		
	INSURANCE		
	MAINTENANCE		
	ELECTRICITY		
	WATER/SEWER		
	GAS/HEATING		
	TRASH		
	PHONE		
	TV/INTERNET		
	SUBTOTAL		
FOOD	GROCERIES		
	DINING OUT		
	SUBTOTAL		
HEALTH CARE	INSURANCE		
	MEDICAL		
	SUBTOTAL		
TRANSPORTATION	CAR PAYMENT		
	INSURANCE		
	FUEL		
	MAINTENANCE		
	PUBLIC TRANS		
	SUBTOTAL		

	EXPENSE	BUDGETED	ACTUAL
PERSONAL	CLOTHING		
	PERSONAL CARE		
	SUBTOTAL		
LOANS	CREDIT CARDS		
	SUBTOTAL		
ENTERTAINMENT	EVENTS/GAMES		
	HOBBIES		
	SUBTOTAL		
OTHER			
	SUBTOTAL		

TOTAL BUDGETED	TOTAL ACTUAL	DIFFERENCE

MONTH 5

EXPENSE TRACKER

DATE	DESCRIPTION	CATEGORY	AMOUNT

MONTH 5

EXPENSE TRACKER

DATE	DESCRIPTION	CATEGORY	AMOUNT

MONTH 5

EXPENSE TRACKER

DATE	DESCRIPTION	CATEGORY	AMOUNT

MONTH 5

EXPENSE TRACKER

DATE	DESCRIPTION	CATEGORY	AMOUNT

MONTH 5

BUDGET REVIEW

OPENING BALANCE	
TOTAL INCOME	
TOTAL EXPENSES	
DIFFERENCE	
TOTAL SAVINGS	
BALANCE FORWARD	

SPENDING ANALYSIS

CATEGORY	AMOUNT	%

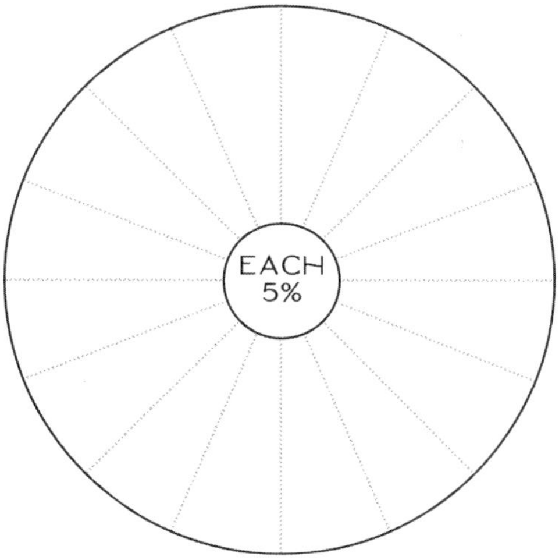

MY BIGGEST WINS THIS MONTH...

DID I MEET MY BUDGET? IF NOT, WHY NOT?

DID I ACHIEVE THIS MONTH'S GOALS? IF NOT, WHY NOT?

WHAT DID I LEARN THIS MONTH FROM TRACKING MY EXPENSES?

MONTH 5

THOUGHTS, NOTES & IDEAS

MONTH 6

MONTH & YEAR:

MAIN GOALS THIS MONTH *in order of priority*

FINANCIAL TO-DO LIST

INCOME	AMOUNT	DATE

SAVINGS	AMOUNT	DATE

SUN	MON	TUE	WED	THU	FRI	SAT

MONTH 6

MONTHLY BUDGET

	EXPENSE	BUDGETED	ACTUAL
HOUSING	MORTAGE/RENT		
	INSURANCE		
	MAINTENANCE		
	ELECTRICITY		
	WATER/SEWER		
	GAS/HEATING		
	TRASH		
	PHONE		
	TV/INTERNET		
	SUBTOTAL		
FOOD	GROCERIES		
	DINING OUT		
	SUBTOTAL		
HEALTH CARE	INSURANCE		
	MEDICAL		
	SUBTOTAL		
TRANSPORTATION	CAR PAYMENT		
	INSURANCE		
	FUEL		
	MAINTENANCE		
	PUBLIC TRANS		
SUBTOTAL			

	EXPENSE	BUDGETED	ACTUAL
PERSONAL	CLOTHING		
	PERSONAL CARE		
	SUBTOTAL		
LOANS	CREDIT CARDS		
	SUBTOTAL		
ENTERTAINMENT	EVENTS/GAMES		
	HOBBIES		
	SUBTOTAL		
OTHER			
SUBTOTAL			

TOTAL BUDGETED	TOTAL ACTUAL	DIFFERENCE

MONTH 6

EXPENSE TRACKER

DATE	DESCRIPTION	CATEGORY	AMOUNT

MONTH 6

EXPENSE TRACKER

DATE	DESCRIPTION	CATEGORY	AMOUNT

MONTH 6

EXPENSE TRACKER

DATE	DESCRIPTION	CATEGORY	AMOUNT

MONTH 6

EXPENSE TRACKER

DATE	DESCRIPTION	CATEGORY	AMOUNT

MONTH 6

BUDGET REVIEW

OPENING BALANCE	
TOTAL INCOME	
TOTAL EXPENSES	
DIFFERENCE	
TOTAL SAVINGS	
BALANCE FORWARD	

SPENDING ANALYSIS

CATEGORY	AMOUNT	%

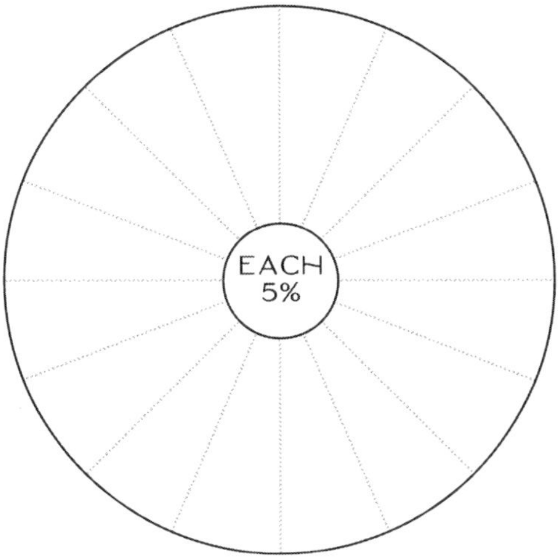

MY BIGGEST WINS THIS MONTH...

DID I MEET MY BUDGET? IF NOT, WHY NOT?

DID I ACHIEVE THIS MONTH'S GOALS? IF NOT, WHY NOT?

WHAT DID I LEARN THIS MONTH FROM TRACKING MY EXPENSES?

MONTH 6
THOUGHTS, NOTES & IDEAS

MONTH 7

MONTH & YEAR:

MAIN GOALS THIS MONTH *in order of priority*

FINANCIAL TO-DO LIST

INCOME	AMOUNT	DATE

SAVINGS	AMOUNT	DATE

SUN	MON	TUE	WED	THU	FRI	SAT

MONTH 7

MONTHLY BUDGET

	EXPENSE	BUDGETED	ACTUAL
HOUSING	MORTAGE/RENT		
	INSURANCE		
	MAINTENANCE		
	ELECTRICITY		
	WATER/SEWER		
	GAS/HEATING		
	TRASH		
	PHONE		
	TV/INTERNET		
	SUBTOTAL		
FOOD	GROCERIES		
	DINING OUT		
	SUBTOTAL		
HEALTH CARE	INSURANCE		
	MEDICAL		
	SUBTOTAL		
TRANSPORTATION	CAR PAYMENT		
	INSURANCE		
	FUEL		
	MAINTENANCE		
	PUBLIC TRANS		
	SUBTOTAL		

	EXPENSE	BUDGETED	ACTUAL
PERSONAL	CLOTHING		
	PERSONAL CARE		
	SUBTOTAL		
LOANS	CREDIT CARDS		
	SUBTOTAL		
ENTERTAINMENT	EVENTS/GAMES		
	HOBBIES		
	SUBTOTAL		
OTHER			
	SUBTOTAL		

TOTAL BUDGETED	TOTAL ACTUAL	DIFFERENCE

MONTH 7

EXPENSE TRACKER

DATE	DESCRIPTION	CATEGORY	AMOUNT

MONTH 7
EXPENSE TRACKER

DATE	DESCRIPTION	CATEGORY	AMOUNT

MONTH 7

EXPENSE TRACKER

DATE	DESCRIPTION	CATEGORY	AMOUNT

MONTH 7

EXPENSE TRACKER

DATE	DESCRIPTION	CATEGORY	AMOUNT

MONTH 7

BUDGET REVIEW

OPENING BALANCE	
TOTAL INCOME	
TOTAL EXPENSES	
DIFFERENCE	
TOTAL SAVINGS	
BALANCE FORWARD	

SPENDING ANALYSIS

CATEGORY	AMOUNT	%

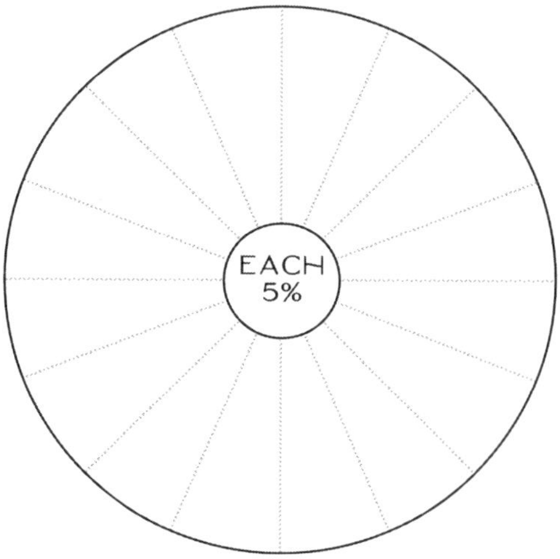

MY BIGGEST WINS THIS MONTH...

DID I MEET MY BUDGET? IF NOT, WHY NOT?

DID I ACHIEVE THIS MONTH'S GOALS? IF NOT, WHY NOT?

WHAT DID I LEARN THIS MONTH FROM TRACKING MY EXPENSES?

MONTH 7

THOUGHTS, NOTES & IDEAS

MONTH 8

MONTH & YEAR:

MAIN GOALS THIS MONTH *in order of priority*

FINANCIAL TO-DO LIST

INCOME	AMOUNT	DATE

SAVINGS	AMOUNT	DATE

SUN	MON	TUE	WED	THU	FRI	SAT

MONTH 8

MONTHLY BUDGET

	EXPENSE	BUDGETED	ACTUAL
HOUSING	MORTAGE/RENT		
	INSURANCE		
	MAINTENANCE		
	ELECTRICITY		
	WATER/SEWER		
	GAS/HEATING		
	TRASH		
	PHONE		
	TV/INTERNET		
	SUBTOTAL		
FOOD	GROCERIES		
	DINING OUT		
	SUBTOTAL		
HEALTH CARE	INSURANCE		
	MEDICAL		
	SUBTOTAL		
TRANSPORTATION	CAR PAYMENT		
	INSURANCE		
	FUEL		
	MAINTENANCE		
	PUBLIC TRANS		
	SUBTOTAL		

	EXPENSE	BUDGETED	ACTUAL
PERSONAL	CLOTHING		
	PERSONAL CARE		
	SUBTOTAL		
LOANS	CREDIT CARDS		
	SUBTOTAL		
ENTERTAINMENT	EVENTS/GAMES		
	HOBBIES		
	SUBTOTAL		
OTHER			
	SUBTOTAL		

TOTAL BUDGETED	TOTAL ACTUAL	DIFFERENCE

MONTH 8

EXPENSE TRACKER

DATE	DESCRIPTION	CATEGORY	AMOUNT

MONTH 8

EXPENSE TRACKER

DATE	DESCRIPTION	CATEGORY	AMOUNT

MONTH 8

EXPENSE TRACKER

DATE	DESCRIPTION	CATEGORY	AMOUNT

MONTH 8

EXPENSE TRACKER

DATE	DESCRIPTION	CATEGORY	AMOUNT

MONTH 8

BUDGET REVIEW

OPENING BALANCE	
TOTAL INCOME	
TOTAL EXPENSES	
DIFFERENCE	
TOTAL SAVINGS	
BALANCE FORWARD	

SPENDING ANALYSIS

CATEGORY	AMOUNT	%

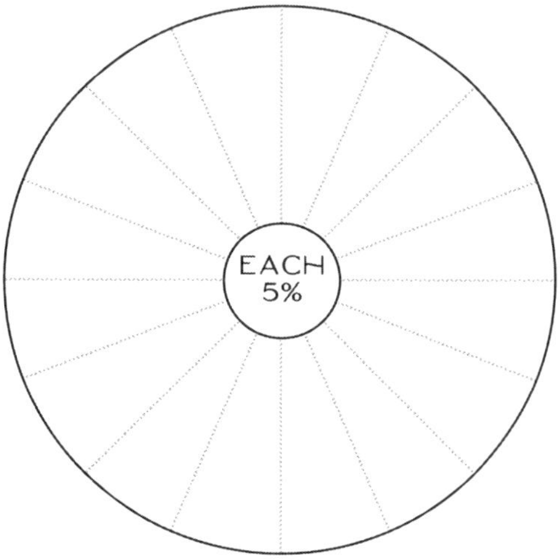

MY BIGGEST WINS THIS MONTH...

DID I MEET MY BUDGET? IF NOT, WHY NOT?

DID I ACHIEVE THIS MONTH'S GOALS? IF NOT, WHY NOT?

WHAT DID I LEARN THIS MONTH FROM TRACKING MY EXPENSES?

MONTH 8

THOUGHTS, NOTES & IDEAS

MONTH & YEAR:

MAIN GOALS THIS MONTH *in order of priority*

FINANCIAL TO-DO LIST

INCOME	AMOUNT	DATE

SAVINGS	AMOUNT	DATE

SUN	MON	TUE	WED	THU	FRI	SAT

MONTH 9

MONTHLY BUDGET

	EXPENSE	BUDGETED	ACTUAL
HOUSING	MORTAGE/RENT		
	INSURANCE		
	MAINTENANCE		
	ELECTRICITY		
	WATER/SEWER		
	GAS/HEATING		
	TRASH		
	PHONE		
	TV/INTERNET		
	SUBTOTAL		
FOOD	GROCERIES		
	DINING OUT		
	SUBTOTAL		
HEALTH CARE	INSURANCE		
	MEDICAL		
	SUBTOTAL		
TRANSPORTATION	CAR PAYMENT		
	INSURANCE		
	FUEL		
	MAINTENANCE		
	PUBLIC TRANS		
	SUBTOTAL		

	EXPENSE	BUDGETED	ACTUAL
PERSONAL	CLOTHING		
	PERSONAL CARE		
	SUBTOTAL		
LOANS	CREDIT CARDS		
	SUBTOTAL		
ENTERTAINMENT	EVENTS/GAMES		
	HOBBIES		
	SUBTOTAL		
OTHER			
	SUBTOTAL		

TOTAL BUDGETED	TOTAL ACTUAL	DIFFERENCE

MONTH 9

EXPENSE TRACKER

DATE	DESCRIPTION	CATEGORY	AMOUNT

MONTH 9

EXPENSE TRACKER

DATE	DESCRIPTION	CATEGORY	AMOUNT

MONTH 9

EXPENSE TRACKER

DATE	DESCRIPTION	CATEGORY	AMOUNT

MONTH 9

EXPENSE TRACKER

DATE	DESCRIPTION	CATEGORY	AMOUNT

MONTH 9

BUDGET REVIEW

OPENING BALANCE	
TOTAL INCOME	
TOTAL EXPENSES	
DIFFERENCE	
TOTAL SAVINGS	
BALANCE FORWARD	

SPENDING ANALYSIS

CATEGORY	AMOUNT	%

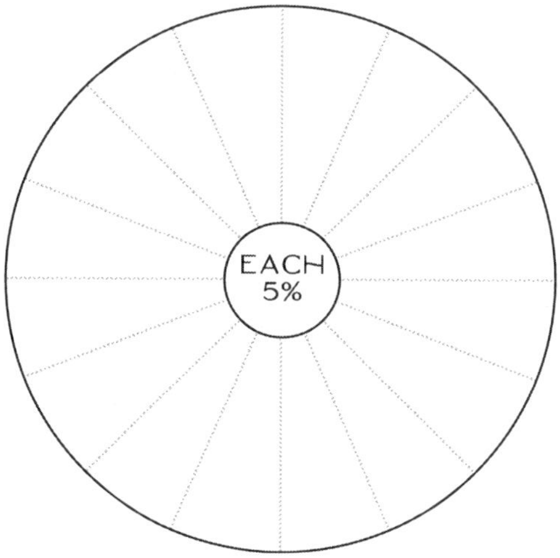

MY BIGGEST WINS THIS MONTH...

DID I MEET MY BUDGET? IF NOT, WHY NOT?

DID I ACHIEVE THIS MONTH'S GOALS? IF NOT, WHY NOT?

WHAT DID I LEARN THIS MONTH FROM TRACKING MY EXPENSES?

MONTH 9

THOUGHTS, NOTES & IDEAS

MONTH 10

MONTH & YEAR:

MAIN GOALS THIS MONTH *in order of priority*

FINANCIAL TO-DO LIST

INCOME	AMOUNT	DATE

SAVINGS	AMOUNT	DATE

SUN	MON	TUE	WED	THU	FRI	SAT

MONTH 10

MONTHLY BUDGET

	EXPENSE	BUDGETED	ACTUAL
HOUSING	MORTAGE/RENT		
	INSURANCE		
	MAINTENANCE		
	ELECTRICITY		
	WATER/SEWER		
	GAS/HEATING		
	TRASH		
	PHONE		
	TV/INTERNET		
	SUBTOTAL		
FOOD	GROCERIES		
	DINING OUT		
	SUBTOTAL		
HEALTH CARE	INSURANCE		
	MEDICAL		
	SUBTOTAL		
TRANSPORTATION	CAR PAYMENT		
	INSURANCE		
	FUEL		
	MAINTENANCE		
	PUBLIC TRANS		
	SUBTOTAL		

	EXPENSE	BUDGETED	ACTUAL
PERSONAL	CLOTHING		
	PERSONAL CARE		
	SUBTOTAL		
LOANS	CREDIT CARDS		
	SUBTOTAL		
ENTERTAINMENT	EVENTS/GAMES		
	HOBBIES		
	SUBTOTAL		
OTHER			
	SUBTOTAL		

TOTAL BUDGETED	TOTAL ACTUAL	DIFFERENCE

MONTH 10

EXPENSE TRACKER

DATE	DESCRIPTION	CATEGORY	AMOUNT

MONTH 10

EXPENSE TRACKER

DATE	DESCRIPTION	CATEGORY	AMOUNT

MONTH 10

EXPENSE TRACKER

DATE	DESCRIPTION	CATEGORY	AMOUNT

MONTH 10

EXPENSE TRACKER

DATE	DESCRIPTION	CATEGORY	AMOUNT

MONTH 10

BUDGET REVIEW

OPENING BALANCE	
TOTAL INCOME	
TOTAL EXPENSES	
DIFFERENCE	
TOTAL SAVINGS	
BALANCE FORWARD	

SPENDING ANALYSIS

CATEGORY	AMOUNT	%

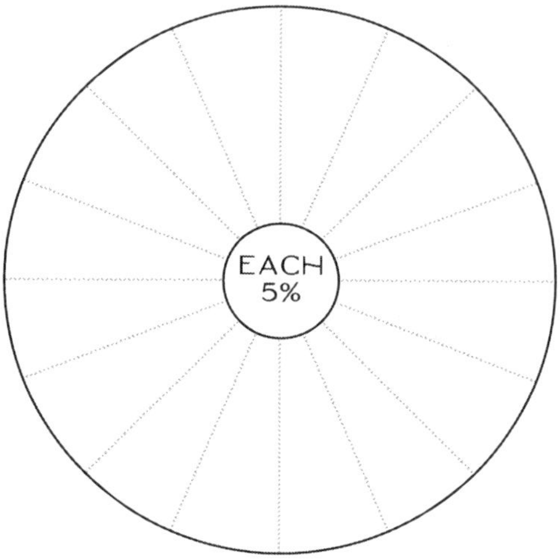

MY BIGGEST WINS THIS MONTH...

DID I MEET MY BUDGET? IF NOT, WHY NOT?

DID I ACHIEVE THIS MONTH'S GOALS? IF NOT, WHY NOT?

WHAT DID I LEARN THIS MONTH FROM TRACKING MY EXPENSES?

MONTH 10

THOUGHTS, NOTES & IDEAS

MONTH & YEAR:

MAIN GOALS THIS MONTH *in order of priority*

FINANCIAL TO-DO LIST

INCOME	AMOUNT	DATE

SAVINGS	AMOUNT	DATE

SUN	MON	TUE	WED	THU	FRI	SAT

MONTH 11

MONTHLY BUDGET

	EXPENSE	BUDGETED	ACTUAL
HOUSING	MORTAGE/RENT		
	INSURANCE		
	MAINTENANCE		
	ELECTRICITY		
	WATER/SEWER		
	GAS/HEATING		
	TRASH		
	PHONE		
	TV/INTERNET		
	SUBTOTAL		
FOOD	GROCERIES		
	DINING OUT		
	SUBTOTAL		
HEALTH CARE	INSURANCE		
	MEDICAL		
	SUBTOTAL		
TRANSPORTATION	CAR PAYMENT		
	INSURANCE		
	FUEL		
	MAINTENANCE		
	PUBLIC TRANS		
	SUBTOTAL		

	EXPENSE	BUDGETED	ACTUAL
PERSONAL	CLOTHING		
	PERSONAL CARE		
	SUBTOTAL		
LOANS	CREDIT CARDS		
	SUBTOTAL		
ENTERTAINMENT	EVENTS/GAMES		
	HOBBIES		
	SUBTOTAL		
OTHER			
	SUBTOTAL		

TOTAL BUDGETED	TOTAL ACTUAL	DIFFERENCE

MONTH 11

EXPENSE TRACKER

DATE	DESCRIPTION	CATEGORY	AMOUNT

MONTH 11

EXPENSE TRACKER

DATE	DESCRIPTION	CATEGORY	AMOUNT

MONTH 11

EXPENSE TRACKER

DATE	DESCRIPTION	CATEGORY	AMOUNT

MONTH 11

EXPENSE TRACKER

DATE	DESCRIPTION	CATEGORY	AMOUNT

MONTH 11

BUDGET REVIEW

OPENING BALANCE	
TOTAL INCOME	
TOTAL EXPENSES	
DIFFERENCE	
TOTAL SAVINGS	
BALANCE FORWARD	

SPENDING ANALYSIS

CATEGORY	AMOUNT	%

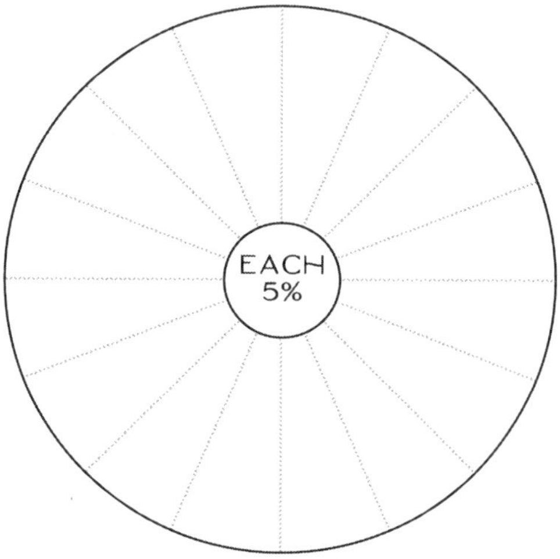

MY BIGGEST WINS THIS MONTH...

DID I MEET MY BUDGET? IF NOT, WHY NOT?

DID I ACHIEVE THIS MONTH'S GOALS? IF NOT, WHY NOT?

WHAT DID I LEARN THIS MONTH FROM TRACKING MY EXPENSES?

MONTH 11

THOUGHTS, NOTES & IDEAS

MONTH 12

MONTH & YEAR:

MAIN GOALS THIS MONTH *in order of priority*

FINANCIAL TO-DO LIST

INCOME	AMOUNT	DATE

SAVINGS	AMOUNT	DATE

SUN	MON	TUE	WED	THU	FRI	SAT

MONTH 12

MONTHLY BUDGET

	EXPENSE	BUDGETED	ACTUAL
HOUSING	MORTAGE/RENT		
	INSURANCE		
	MAINTENANCE		
	ELECTRICITY		
	WATER/SEWER		
	GAS/HEATING		
	TRASH		
	PHONE		
	TV/INTERNET		
	SUBTOTAL		
FOOD	GROCERIES		
	DINING OUT		
	SUBTOTAL		
HEALTH CARE	INSURANCE		
	MEDICAL		
	SUBTOTAL		
TRANSPORTATION	CAR PAYMENT		
	INSURANCE		
	FUEL		
	MAINTENANCE		
	PUBLIC TRANS		
	SUBTOTAL		

	EXPENSE	BUDGETED	ACTUAL
PERSONAL	CLOTHING		
	PERSONAL CARE		
	SUBTOTAL		
LOANS	CREDIT CARDS		
	SUBTOTAL		
ENTERTAINMENT	EVENTS/GAMES		
	HOBBIES		
	SUBTOTAL		
OTHER			
	SUBTOTAL		

TOTAL BUDGETED	TOTAL ACTUAL	DIFFERENCE

MONTH 12

EXPENSE TRACKER

DATE	DESCRIPTION	CATEGORY	AMOUNT

MONTH 12

EXPENSE TRACKER

DATE	DESCRIPTION	CATEGORY	AMOUNT

MONTH 12

EXPENSE TRACKER

DATE	DESCRIPTION	CATEGORY	AMOUNT

MONTH 12

EXPENSE TRACKER

DATE	DESCRIPTION	CATEGORY	AMOUNT

MONTH 12

BUDGET REVIEW

OPENING BALANCE	
TOTAL INCOME	
TOTAL EXPENSES	
DIFFERENCE	
TOTAL SAVINGS	
BALANCE FORWARD	

SPENDING ANALYSIS

CATEGORY	AMOUNT	%

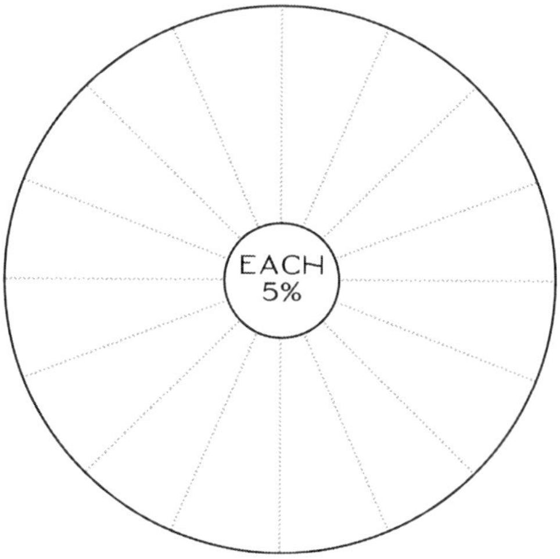

MY BIGGEST WINS THIS MONTH...

DID I MEET MY BUDGET? IF NOT, WHY NOT?

DID I ACHIEVE THIS MONTH'S GOALS? IF NOT, WHY NOT?

WHAT DID I LEARN THIS MONTH FROM TRACKING MY EXPENSES?

MONTH 12

THOUGHTS, NOTES & IDEAS

SAVINGS TRACKER

SAVING FOR	AMOUNT NEEDED	DUE DATE

DATE	DEPOSIT	BALANCE

SAVING FOR	AMOUNT NEEDED	DUE DATE

DATE	DEPOSIT	BALANCE

SAVINGS TRACKER

SAVING FOR	AMOUNT NEEDED	DUE DATE

DATE	DEPOSIT	BALANCE

SAVING FOR	AMOUNT NEEDED	DUE DATE

DATE	DEPOSIT	BALANCE

SAVINGS TRACKER

SAVING FOR	AMOUNT NEEDED	DUE DATE

DATE	DEPOSIT	BALANCE

SAVING FOR	AMOUNT NEEDED	DUE DATE

DATE	DEPOSIT	BALANCE

EMERGENCY FUND

SAVINGS TRACKER

SAVING FOR	AMOUNT NEEDED	DUE DATE

DATE	DEPOSIT	BALANCE

SAVING FOR	AMOUNT NEEDED	DUE DATE

DATE	DEPOSIT	BALANCE

DEBT TRACKER

DEBT NAME	STARTING BALANCE	MINIMUM PAYMENT

DATE	AMOUNT PAID	BALANCE

DEBT NAME	STARTING BALANCE	MINIMUM PAYMENT

DATE	AMOUNT PAID	BALANCE

DEBT TRACKER

DEBT NAME	STARTING BALANCE	MINIMUM PAYMENT

DATE	AMOUNT PAID	BALANCE

DEBT NAME	STARTING BALANCE	MINIMUM PAYMENT

DATE	AMOUNT PAID	BALANCE

DEBT TRACKER

DEBT NAME	STARTING BALANCE	MINIMUM PAYMENT

DATE	AMOUNT PAID	BALANCE

DEBT NAME	STARTING BALANCE	MINIMUM PAYMENT

DATE	AMOUNT PAID	BALANCE

DEBT TRACKER

DEBT NAME	STARTING BALANCE	MINIMUM PAYMENT

DATE	AMOUNT PAID	BALANCE

DEBT NAME	STARTING BALANCE	MINIMUM PAYMENT

DATE	AMOUNT PAID	BALANCE

DEBT TRACKER

DEBT NAME	STARTING BALANCE	MINIMUM PAYMENT

DATE	AMOUNT PAID	BALANCE

DEBT NAME	STARTING BALANCE	MINIMUM PAYMENT

DATE	AMOUNT PAID	BALANCE

DEBT TRACKER

DEBT NAME	STARTING BALANCE	MINIMUM PAYMENT

DATE	AMOUNT PAID	BALANCE

DEBT NAME	STARTING BALANCE	MINIMUM PAYMENT

DATE	AMOUNT PAID	BALANCE

REGULAR BILL TRACKER

BILL MONTH →						

REGULAR BILL TRACKER

BILL / MONTH →						

SUMMARY OF THE YEAR

MONTH						
INCOME						
EXPENSES						
DIFFERENCE						
SAVINGS						

MONTHLY EXPENSES SUMMARY

CATEGORY						
HOUSING						
FOOD						
HEALTH CARE						
TRANSPORTATION						
PERSONAL						
LOANS						
ENTERTAINMENT						

SUMMARY OF THE YEAR

MONTH						
INCOME						
EXPENSES						
DIFFERENCE						
SAVINGS						

MONTHLY EXPENSES SUMMARY

CATEGORY

HOUSING						
FOOD						
HEALTH CARE						
TRANSPORTATION						
PERSONAL						
LOANS						
ENTERTAINMENT						

PASSWORD TRACKER

NAME ACCOUNT
WEBSITE USERNAME
PASSWORD
NOTES

NAME ACCOUNT
WEBSITE USERNAME
PASSWORD
NOTES

NAME ACCOUNT
WEBSITE USERNAME
PASSWORD
NOTES

NAME ACCOUNT
WEBSITE USERNAME
PASSWORD
NOTES

NAME ACCOUNT
WEBSITE USERNAME
PASSWORD
NOTES

NAME ACCOUNT
WEBSITE USERNAME
PASSWORD
NOTES

PASSWORD TRACKER

NAME ACCOUNT
WEBSITE USERNAME
PASSWORD
NOTES

NAME ACCOUNT
WEBSITE USERNAME
PASSWORD
NOTES

NAME ACCOUNT
WEBSITE USERNAME
PASSWORD
NOTES

NAME ACCOUNT
WEBSITE USERNAME
PASSWORD
NOTES

NAME ACCOUNT
WEBSITE USERNAME
PASSWORD
NOTES

NAME ACCOUNT
WEBSITE USERNAME
PASSWORD
NOTES

TOP SIDE HUSTLES FOR EXTRA INCOME

TO CREATE THIS YEAR

- ★ DELIVERY: PACKAGE, GROCERY, AND/OR FOOD DELIVERY SERVICES
- ★ ONLINE TUTORING
- ★ VIRTUAL ASSISTANT
- ★ FREELANCE WORK
- ★ OTHER IDEAS

TIME SAVING HABITS

TIME IS MONEY

- ★ PLAN AND PREPARE AHEAD OF TIME.
- ★ HANDLE SMALL TASKS RIGHT AWAY SO THEY DON'T BUILD UP
- ★ BLOCK OFF TIME TO GET TASKS AND WORK DONE
- ★ LIMIT SCREEN TIME AND AVOID SCROLLING
- ★ BECOME A MINIMALIST WHERE YOU CAN THE MORE YOU HAVE, THE MORE YOU HAVE TO MANAGE.
- ★ RE-EVALUATE YOUR PRIORITIES

INSPIRATIONAL QUOTES

WHICH RESONATES MOST WITH YOU?

DO NOT SAVE WHAT IS LEFT AFTER SPENDING,
BUT SPEND WHAT IS LEFT AFTER SAVING.

WARREN BUFFET

DON'T GO BROKE TRYING TO LOOK RICH

WEALTH CONSISTS NOT IN HAVING GREAT
POSSESSIONS, BUT IN HAVING FEW WANTS

EPICTETUS

TOO MANY PEOPLE SPEND MONEY THEY HAVEN'T EARNED
TO BUY THINGS THEY DON'T WANT, TO IMPRESS PEOPLE
THAT THEY DON'T LIKE.

WILL ROGERS

THE MORE MONEY WORKS FOR YOU,
THE LESS YOU HAVE TO WORK FOR MONEY.

IDOWU KOYENIKAN

MY FAVORITE QUOTES

Made in United States
North Haven, CT
05 November 2026

21772054R00078